Our Town

Shopping List

Yarn
- ☐ (Medium Weight) 4 approximately 20-30 yards (18.5-27.5 cm) (see photos for color suggestions)

Crochet Hook
- ☐ Size F (3.75 mm) **or size needed for gauge**

Additional Supplies
- ☐ Yarn needle
- ☐ Ribbon, 7 mm moveable eyes, 7 mm pom-poms, beads, wire, glue gun, and purchased miniature accessories were used for finishing

Gauge Information
8 sc = 2" (5 cm)

EASY

TABLE OF CONTENTS

All the time, children are asked what they want to be when they grow up, and every time, their answer will be different. They want to be doctors, astronauts, teachers, artists, police officers, or something else. Their dreams are wild and endless. The citizens of Our Town work all different occupations, and your little one will get the chance to create and hang out with Finger Puppets like Zander – the artist, or Andre – the Chief. All designs are crocheted using worsted weight yarn and a Size F (3.75 mm) crochet hook.

LEISURE ARTS, INC. • Maumelle, Arkansas

the Teacher

When you're having a hard day at school, your favorite teacher will be your best friend. Gertrude, the teacher, loves school, but she loves her students even more. From adding numbers to writing words, Gertrude will make the hard work so much easier! Make sure to leave her a juicy, apple on her desk Monday morning.

Gertrude

Body

With Peach, ch 4 **loosely**; being careful **not** to twist ch, join with slip st to form a ring.

Rnd 1 (RS): Ch 1, 2 sc in same ch as joining and in each ch around; do **not** join, place marker to indicate the beginning of the rnd **(see Markers, page 18)**: 8 sc.

Rnd 2: 2 Sc in each sc around: 16 sc.

Rnds 3-5: Sc in each sc around.

Rnd 6: (Skip next sc, sc in next sc) around: 8 sc.

Rnd 7: Sc in each sc around, changing to Rose in last sc **(Fig. 2, page 19)**.

Rnds 8-10: Sc in each sc around.

Rnd 11: ★ Sc in next sc, ch 9 **loosely**, do **not** cut Rose; with Peach, ch 2, 4 hdc in second ch from hook, changing to Rose in last hdc made; hdc in next 9 chs, slip st in same st as last sc worked; repeat from ★ once **more**, sc in next 6 sc, slip st in next sc; finish off.

Finishing

Hair: Cut a piece of cardboard 2" (5 cm) square. Wind a strand of Brown yarn around the cardboard approximately 16 times. Cut a 6" (15 cm) length of Brown yarn and insert it under all of the strands at the top of the cardboard; pull up **tightly** and tie securely. Cut the yarn at the opposite end of the cardboard and then remove it. Cut a 6" (15 cm) length of Rose yarn and wrap it **tightly** around the tassel once, $\frac{3}{8}$" (9.5 mm) below the top; tie securely. Unravel cut ends, glue to top of head and trim.

Use photos as a guide for shaping and for placement of features and accessories.

theChief

Cooking in his own restaurant has been his dream since he was a small kid. Andrew knows how to cook up the best meal anyone has ever tasted. Interested? He has multiple cooking books for sale that you should buy and try. What are you going to whip up today?

Andre

Body

With Peach, ch 4 **loosely**; being careful **not** to twist ch, join with slip st to form a ring.

Rnd 1 (RS): Ch 1, 2 sc in same ch as joining and in each ch around; do **not** join, place marker to indicate the beginning of the rnd **(see Markers, page 18)**: 8 sc.

Rnd 2: 2 Sc in each sc around: 16 sc.

Rnds 3-5: Sc in each sc around.

Rnd 6: (Skip next sc, sc in next sc) around: 8 sc.

Rnd 7: Sc in each sc around, changing to White in last sc **(Fig. 2, page 19)**.

Rnds 8-10: Sc in each sc around.

Rnd 11: ★ Sc in next sc, ch 9 **loosely**, do **not** cut White; with Peach, ch 2, 4 hdc in second ch from hook, changing to White in last hdc made; hdc in next 9 chs, slip st in same st as last sc worked; repeat from ★ once **more**, sc in next 6 sc, slip st in next sc; finish off.

Hat

With White, ch 16 **loosely**; being careful **not** to twist ch, join with slip st to form a ring.

Rnd 1 (RS): Ch 1, sc in same ch as joining and in each ch around; do **not** join, place marker to indicate the beginning of the rnd: 16 sc.

Rnds 2 and 3: Sc in each sc around.

Rnd 4: (Sc in next sc, 2 sc in next sc) around: 24 sc.

Rnds 5 and 6: Sc in each sc around.

Rnd 7: (Skip next sc, sc in next 2 sc) around: 16 sc.

Rnd 8: (Skip next sc, sc in next sc) around: 8 sc.

Rnd 9: (Skip next sc, slip st in next sc) around; finish off .

Scarf

Row 1: With Red, ch 2, 3 sc in second ch from hook: 3 sc.

Row 2: Ch 1, turn; sc in each sc across.

Row 3: Ch 1, turn; 2 sc in first sc, sc in next sc, 2 sc in last sc: 5 sc.

Row 4: Ch 1, turn; sc in each sc across, ch 8, place around neck (Rnd 7) and slip st in first sc to join; finish off.

Finishing

Moustache: Cut two 2" (5 cm) strands of Black yarn. Add one strand of fringe at a time to center of head on Rnd 5 **(Figs. 5a & b, page 21)**. Unravel and trim ends.

Use photo as a guide for shaping and for placement of features and accessories.

the Fireman

Fires are no match for your favorite Firefighter. Carl and his trusty team calm the blaze in a matter of minutes. He'll be the hero you can call. The hero you can count on.

Carl

Body

With Peach, ch 4 **loosely**; being careful **not** to twist ch, join with slip st to form a ring.

Rnd 1 (RS): Ch 1, 2 sc in same ch as joining and in each ch around; do **not** join, place marker to indicate the beginning of the rnd **(see Markers, page 18)**: 8 sc.

Rnd 2: 2 Sc in each sc around: 16 sc.

Rnds 3-5: Sc in each sc around.

Rnd 6: (Skip next sc, sc in next sc) around: 8 sc.

Rnd 7: Sc in each sc around, changing to Red in last sc **(Fig. 2, page 19)**.

Rnds 8-10: Sc in each sc around.

Rnd 11: ★ Sc in next sc, ch 9 **loosely**, do **not** cut Red; with Peach, ch 2, 4 hdc in second ch from hook, changing to Red in last hdc made; hdc in next 9 chs, slip st in same st as last sc worked ; repeat from ★ once **more**, changing to Black in last slip st made; sc in next 6 sc, ch 10; keeping ch in front of arm, slip st in next sc (between arms), ch 10; keeping ch in front of arm, slip st in next sc; finish off.

Hat

With Red, ch 4 **loosely**; being careful **not** to twist ch, join with slip st to form a ring.

Rnd 1 (RS): Ch 1, 2 sc in same ch as joining and in each ch around; do **not** join, place marker to indicate the beginning of the rnd: 8 sc.

Rnd 2: 2 Sc in each sc around: 16 sc.

Rnds 3-5: Sc in each sc around.

Rnd 6: Working in FLO **(Fig. 1, page 19)**, ★ (sc, hdc) in next sc, 2 dc in next sc, 2 tr in next sc, 2 dc in next sc, (hdc, sc) in next sc, sc in next 3 sc; repeat from ★ once **more**, slip st in both loops of next sc; finish off.

Hose

Row 1: With Ecru, ch 26 **loosely**; hdc in third ch from hook and in each ch across; finish off.
Make a 1" (2.5 cm) cone with silver foil. Glue end of hose inside cone.

Finishing

Moustache: Cut two 2" (5 cm) strands of Brown yarn. Add one strand of fringe at a time to center of head on Rnd 5 **(Figs. 5a & b, page 21)**. Unravel and trim ends.

Use photo as a guide for shaping and for placement of features and accessories.

the Artist

There's an artist inside all of us, even you. Whether you paint or write, every art piece you create will be perfect. Now become the artist you dream of, just like Zander!

Zander

Body

With Red, ch 4 **loosely**; being careful **not** to twist ch, join with slip st to form a ring.

Rnd 1: Ch 1, work 2 Loop Sts in each ch around **(Figs. 4a-c, page 21)**; do **not** join, place marker to indicate the beginning of the rnd **(see Markers, page 18)**: 8 Loop Sts.

Rnd 2: Work 2 Loop Sts in each st around: 16 Loop Sts.

Rnd 3: Work Loop St in next 4 sts, changing to Peach in last Loop St made **(Fig. 2, page 19)**; sc in each st around.

Rnds 4 and 5: Sc in each sc around.

Rnd 6: (Skip next sc, sc in next sc) around: 8 sc.

Rnd 7: Sc in each sc around, changing to Variegated in last sc.

Rnds 8-10: Sc in each sc around.

Rnd 11: ★ Sc in next sc, ch 9 **loosely**, do **not** cut Variegated; with Peach, ch 2, 4 hdc in second ch from hook, changing to Variegated in last hdc made; hdc in next 9 chs, slip st in same st as last sc worked; repeat from ★ once **more**, sc in next 6 sc, slip st in next sc; finish off.

Beret

With Variegated, ch 4 **loosely**; being careful **not** to twist ch, join with slip st to form a ring.

Rnd 1 (RS): Ch 1, 2 sc in same ch as joining and in each ch around; do **not** join, place marker to indicate the beginning of the rnd: 8 sc.

Rnd 2: 2 Sc in each sc around: 16 sc.

Rnd 3: (Sc in next sc, 2 sc in next sc) around: 24 sc.

Rnds 4 and 5: Sc in each sc around.

Rnd 6: Working in BLO **(Fig. 1, page 19)**, slip st in each sc around; finish off.

Finishing

Use photo as a guide for shaping and for placement of features and accessories, gluing hair in place where necessary.

theSecretary

Order and organize, Nancy saves lives too. Need help handling a busy schedule? No problem, she will make it happen in a blink of an eye. Nancy already has your planner filled out. Are you in dire need of coffee? Never fear, Nancy heard your yawn and has a cup in hand before you even ask! Never doubt the power of the Secretary because she's the real reason why your day is running so smoothly.

Nancy

Body

With Brown, ch 4 **loosely**; being careful **not** to twist ch, join with slip st to form a ring.

Rnd 1: Ch 1, work 2 Loop Sts in each ch around **(Figs. 4a-c, page 21)**; do **not** join, place marker to indicate the beginning of the rnd **(see Markers, page 18)**: 8 Loop Sts.

Rnd 2: Work 2 Loop Sts in each st around: 16 Loop Sts.

Rnd 3: Work Loop St in next 4 sts, changing to Peach in last Loop St made **(Fig. 2, page 19)**; sc in each st around.

Rnds 4 and 5: Sc in each sc around.

Rnd 6: (Skip next sc, sc in next sc) around: 8 sc.

Rnd 7: Sc in each sc around, changing to Purple in last sc.

Rnds 8-10: Sc in each sc around.

Rnd 11: ★ Sc in next sc, ch 9 **loosely**, do **not** cut Purple; with Peach, ch 2, 4 hdc in second ch from hook, changing to Purple in last hdc made; hdc in next 9 chs, slip st in same st as last sc worked; repeat from ★ once **more**, sc in next 6 sc, slip st in next sc; finish off.

Finishing

Pencils: Cut 1½" (4 cm) lengths from three round wooden toothpicks and use markers to color.

Note Pad: Cut five ⅞" x 3" (2.25 cm x 7.5 cm) strips of paper. Fold in half and staple at fold. Turn first page back and glue in place.

Use photo as a guide for shaping and for placement of features and accessories, gluing hair in place where necessary.

the Paper Boy

Want to read the news? How about finding a job or what the times are for the movies playing at the local movie theater down the street? Don't worry, your favorite Paper Boy, Charly, has your daily paper. He'll arrive at 6 A.M. sharp! If you see him, make sure to wave hello.

Charly

Body

With Peach, ch 4 **loosely**; being careful **not** to twist ch, join with slip st to form a ring.

Rnd 1 (RS): Ch 1, 2 sc in same ch as joining and in each ch around; do **not** join, place marker to indicate the beginning of the rnd **(see Markers, page 18)**: 8 sc.

Rnd 2: 2 Sc in each sc around: 16 sc.

Rnds 3-5: Sc in each sc around.

Rnd 6: (Skip next sc, sc in next sc) around: 8 sc.

Rnd 7: Sc in each sc around, changing to Lt Green in last sc **(Fig. 2, page 19)**.

Rnds 8-10: Sc in each sc around.

Rnd 11: ★ Sc in next sc, ch 9 **loosely**, do **not** cut Lt Green; with Peach, ch 2, 4 hdc in second ch from hook, changing to Lt Green in last hdc made; hdc in next 9 chs, slip st in same st as last sc worked; repeat from ★ once **more**, sc in next 6 sc, slip st in next sc; finish off.

Cap

With Red, ch 4 **loosely**; being careful **not** to twist ch, join with slip st to form a ring.

Rnd 1 (RS): Ch 1, 2 sc in same ch as joining and in each ch around; do **not** join, place marker to indicate the beginning of the rnd: 8 sc.

Rnd 2: 2 Sc in each sc around: 16 sc.

Rnds 3 and 4: Sc in each sc around.

Rnd 5: Working in FLO **(Fig. 1, page 19)**, (sc, hdc) in next sc, 2 dc in each of next 2 sc, (hdc, sc) in next sc, working in both loops, slip st in each sc around; finish off.

Newspaper Bag

With Ecru, ch 4 **loosely**; being careful **not** to twist ch, join with slip st to form a ring.

Rnd 1 (RS): Ch 1, 2 sc in same ch as joining and in each ch around; do **not** join, place marker to indicate the beginning of the rnd: 8 sc.

Rnd 2: 2 Sc in each sc around: 16 sc.

Rnds 3-5: Sc in each sc around.

Rnd 6: Sc in each sc around, ch 12, skip next 7 sc, slip st in next sc; finish off.

Finishing

Newspapers: Cut several 1½" x 2½" (4 cm x 6.5 cm) pieces from movie/television listings of newspaper (smaller print). Fold and put in bag.

Hair: Cut two 2" (5 cm) strands of Brown yarn. Add one strand of fringe at a time to top of head **(Figs. 5a& b, page 21)**. Unravel and trim ends.

Use photo as a guide for shaping and for placement of features and accessories.

the Policeman

No fear! Your favorite policeman is here! Mike will protect you, your friends, your home, and your neighborhood. He'll even help you find your lost pets! Mike, the Policeman, will always have your back.

Mike

Body

With Peach, ch 4 **loosely**; being careful **not** to twist ch, join with slip st to form a ring.

Rnd 1: Ch 1, 2 sc in same ch as joining and in each ch around; do **not** join, place marker to indicate the beginning of the rnd **(see Markers, page 18)**: 8 sc.

Rnd 2: 2 Sc in each sc around: 16 sc.

Rnds 3-5: Sc in each sc around.

Rnd 6: (Skip next sc, sc in next sc) around: 8 sc.

Rnd 7: Sc in each sc around, changing to Blue in last sc **(Fig. 2, page 19)**.

Rnds 8-10: Sc in each sc around.

Rnd 11: ★ Sc in next sc, ch 9 **loosely**, do **not** cut Blue; with Peach, ch 2, 4 hdc in second ch from hook, changing to Blue in last hdc made; hdc in next 9 chs, slip st in same st as last sc worked; repeat from ★ once **more**, sc in next 6 sc, slip st in next sc; finish off.

Cap

With Blue, ch 4 **loosely**; being careful **not** to twist ch, join with slip st to form a ring.

Rnd 1: Ch 1, 2 sc in same ch as joining and in each ch around; do **not** join, place marker to indicate the beginning of the rnd: 8 sc.

Rnd 2: 2 Sc in each sc around: 16 sc.

Rnds 3 and 4: Sc in each sc around; at end of Rnd 4 change to Black in last sc.

Rnd 5: Working in BLO **(Fig. 1, page 19)**, (sc, hdc) in next sc, 2 hdc in next sc, (hdc, sc) in next sc, slip st in each sc around; finish off.

Finishing

Moustache: Cut two 2" (5 cm) strands of Brown yarn. Add one strand of fringe at a time to center of head on Rnd 5 **(Figs. 5a & b, page 21)**. Unravel and trim ends.

Use photo as a guide for shaping and for placement of features and accessories.

the Handyman

Broken faucet? Joe has your back. Has your roof sprung a leak? Joe will patch it right up. Don't worry! He's the best Handyman in the business. The whole town recommends his services.

Joe

Use photo as a guide for shaping and for placement of features and accessories.

Body

With Peach, ch 4 **loosely**; being careful **not** to twist ch, join with slip st to form a ring.

Rnd 1 (RS): Ch 1, 2 sc in same ch as joining and in each ch around; do **not** join, place marker to indicate the beginning of the rnd **(see Markers, page 18)**: 8 sc.

Rnd 2: 2 Sc in each sc around: 16 sc.

Rnds 3-5: Sc in each sc around.

Rnd 6: (Skip next sc, sc in next sc) around: 8 sc.

Rnd 7: Sc in each sc around, changing to Blue in last sc **(Fig. 2, page 19)**.

Rnds 8-10: Sc in each sc around.

Rnd 11: ★ Sc in next sc, ch 9 **loosely**, do **not** cut Blue; with Peach, ch 2, 4 hdc in second ch from hook, changing to Blue in last hdc made; hdc in next 9 chs, slip st in same st as last sc worked; repeat from ★ once **more**, changing to Brown in last slip st made; sc in next 2 sc, (ch 2, sc in next sc) twice, ch 2, sc in next 2 sc, slip st in next sc; finish off.

Hard Hat

With Yellow, ch 4 **loosely**; being careful **not** to twist ch, join with slip st to form a ring.

Rnd 1 (RS): Ch 1, 2 sc in each ch around; do **not** join, place marker to indicate the beginning of the rnd: 8 sc.

Rnd 2: 2 Sc in each sc around: 16 sc.

Rnds 3 and 4: Sc in each sc around.

Rnd 5: Working in FLO **(Fig. 1, page 19)**, (sc, hdc) in next sc, 2 hdc in next sc, (hdc, sc) in next sc, working in both loops, slip st in each sc around; finish off.

Finishing

Moustache: Cut two 2" (5 cm) strands of Black yarn. Add one strand of fringe at a time to center of head on Rnd 5 **(Figs. 5a & b, page 21)**. Unravel and trim ends.

Hair: Cut four 2" (5 cm) strands of Black yarn. Add one strand of fringe at a time to top of head. Unravel and trim ends.

the Cleaning Lady

No matter how big the spill or how crazy the mess, Cassie is the very best. Starting her own cleaning company at the age of eighteen (18), Cassie will make any dirty area spotless in a matter of minutes. Do you enjoy cleaning too?

Cassie

Body

With Peach, ch 4 **loosely**; being careful **not** to twist ch, join with slip st to form a ring.

Rnd 1 (RS): Ch 1, 2 sc in same ch as joining and in each ch around; do **not** join, place marker to indicate the beginning of the rnd **(see Markers, page 18)**: 8 sc.

Rnd 2: 2 Sc in each sc around: 16 sc.

Rnds 3-5: Sc in each sc around.

Rnd 6: (Skip next sc, sc in next sc) around: 8 sc.

Rnd 7: Sc in each sc around, changing to Green in last sc **(Fig. 2, page 19)**.

Rnds 8-10: Sc in each sc around.

Rnd 11: ★ Scin next sc, ch 9 **loosely**, do **not** cut Green; with Peach, ch 2, 4 hdc in second ch from hook, changing to Green in last hdc made; hdc in next 9 chs, slip st in same st as last sc worked; repeat from ★ once **more**, changing to White in last slip st made; sc in next sc, (ch 1, sc in next sc) 5 times, ch 10; keeping ch in front of arm, slip st in next sc (between arms), ch 10; keeping ch in front of arm, slip st in next sc; finish off.

Kerchief

Row 1: With Yellow, ch 2, 3 sc in second ch from hook: 3 sc.

Rows 2-9: Ch 1, turn; 2 sc in first sc, sc in each sc across to last sc, 2 sc in last sc: 19 sc.

Row 10: Ch 1, turn; 2 sc in first sc, sc in each sc across to last sc, 2 sc in last sc, slip st in free loop of beginning ch **(Fig. 3b, page 19) and** in first sc of **Row 10;** finish off.

Finishing

Hair: Cut two 2" (5 cm) strands of Brown yarn. Add one strand of fringe at a time to top of head **(Figs. 5a & b, page 21)**. Unravel and trim ends.

Use photo as a guide for shaping and for placement of features and accessories.

the Boy

Randy loves the outdoors, camping, video games, skateboarding, and so much more. He is the coolest dude in school, but he definitely will stop to say "hello" or lend a helping hand. How sweet! We adore Randy so much.

Randy

Body

With Peach, ch 4 **loosely**; being careful **not** to twist ch, join with slip st to form a ring.

Rnd 1: Ch 1, 2 sc in same ch as joining and in each ch around; do **not** join, place marker to indicate the beginning of the rnd **(see Markers, page 18)**: 8 sc.

Rnd 2: 2 Sc in each sc around: 16 sc.

Rnds 3-5: Sc in each sc around.

Rnd 6: (Skip next sc, sc in next sc) around: 8 sc.

Rnd 7: Sc in each sc around, changing to Yellow in last sc **(Fig. 2, page 19)**.

Rnd 8: Sc in each sc around, changing to White in last sc.

Rnd 9: Sc in each sc around, changing to Yellow in last sc.

Rnd 10: Sc in each sc around.

Rnd 11: ★ Sc in next sc, ch 9 **loosely**, do **not** cut Yellow; with Peach, ch 2, 4 hdc in second ch from hook, changing to Yellow in last hdc made; hdc in next 9 chs, slip st in same st as last sc worked; repeat from ★ once **more**, sc in next 6 sc, slip st in next sc; finish off.

Cap

With Blue, ch 4 **loosely**; being careful not to twist ch, join with slip st to form a ring.

Rnd 1: Ch 1, 2 sc in same ch as joining and in each each ch around; do **not** join, place marker to indicate the beginning of the rnd: 8 sc.

Rnd 2: 2 Sc in each sc around: 16 sc.

Rnds 3 and 4: Sc in each sc around.

Rnd 5: Working in FLO **(Fig. 1, page 19)**, (sc, hdc) in next sc, 2 hdc in each of next 2 sc, (hdc, sc) in next sc, sc in both loops of next 11 sc, slip st in next sc; finish off.

Finishing

Hair: Cut two 2" (5 cm) strands of Brown yarn. Add one strand of fringe at a time to top of head **(Fig. 5b, page 21)**. Unravel and trim ends.

Use photo as a guide for shaping and for placement of features and accessories.

the Blond Girl

Jill is your best friend but also the smartest girl in your class. She'll help you with all your homework or studying for that really hard exam that is approaching. After you and Jill are done with all that school work, she'll kick the winning homerun in Kickball during P.E. There is nothing that Jill can't do.

Jill

Body

With Yellow, ch 4 **loosely**; being careful **not** to twist ch, join with slip st to form a ring.

Rnd 1: Ch 1, work 2 Loop Sts in same st as joining and in each ch around **(Figs. 4a-c, page 21)**; do **not** join, place marker to indicate the beginning of the rnd **(see Markers, page 18)**: 8 Loop Sts.

Rnd 2: Work 2 Loop Sts in each st around: 16 Loop Sts.

Rnd 3: Work Loop St in next 8 sts pulling each loop to measure approximately 1½" (4 cm) and changing to Peach in last Loop St made **(Fig. 2, page 19)**; sc in each st around.

Rnds 4 and 5: Sc in each st around.

Rnd 6: (Skip next sc, sc in next sc) around: 8 sc.

Rnd 7: Sc in each sc around, changing to White in last sc.

Rnd 8 (Collar): Working in BLO **(Fig. 1, page 19)**, (slip st in next sc, ch 3) 7 times, with Blue slip st in next sc.

Rnd 9: Working in free loops on Rnd 7 **(Fig. 3a, page 19)**, sc in each sc around.

Rnds 10 and 11: Working in both loops, sc in each sc around.

Rnd 12: Sc in next 3 sc, † ch 9 **loosely**, do **not** cut Blue; with Peach, ch 2, 4 hdc in second ch from hook, changing to Blue in last hdc made; hdc in next 9 chs, slip st in same st as last sc worked †, sc in next sc, repeat from † to † once, sc in next 4 sc, slip st in next sc; finish off.

Finishing

Hair: Tie a ⅛" (3 mm) ribbon around four 1½" (4 cm) loops on each side of head.

Use photos as a guide for shaping and for placement of features and accessories.

the Teenager

Girls just want to have fun! With hair, make up, all kinds of different outfits, Breanna always has a good time. Her favorite activities are Pumpkin Spice Lattes on a park bench, wearing cardigans, and hanging with her closest friends.

Breanna

Body

With Yellow, ch 4 **loosely**; being careful **not** to twist ch, join with slip st to form a ring.

Rnd 1: Ch 1, work 2 Loop Sts in same ch as joining and in each ch around **(Figs. 4a-c, page 21)**; do **not** join, place marker to indicate the beginning of the rnd **(see Markers, page 18)**: 8 Loop Sts.

Rnd 2: Work 2 Loop Sts in each st around pulling each loop to measure approximately 2" (5 cm): 16 Loop Sts.

Rnd 3: Work Loop St in next 8 sts pulling each loop to measure approximately 2" (5 cm) and changing to Peach in last Loop St made **(Fig. 2, page 19)**, sc in each st around.

Rnds 4 and 5: Sc in each st around.

Rnd 6: (Skip next sc, sc in next sc) around: 8 sc.

Rnd 7: Sc in each sc around, changing to Blue in last sc.

Rnds 8-10: Sc in each sc around.

Rnd 11: Sc in next 3 sc, † ch 9 **loosely**, do **not** cut Blue; with Peach, ch 2, 4 hdc in second ch from hook, changing to Blue in last hdc made; hdc in next 9 chs, slip st in same st as last sc worked †, sc in next sc, repeat from † to † once, sc in next 4 sc, slip st in next sc; finish off.

Finishing

Headband: With Blue ch 20; being careful **not** to twist ch, join with slip st to form a ring, finish off.

Use photos as a guide for shaping and for placement of features and accessories.

☺

theCat

You've tried and tried to convince Mom and Dad that you need a new pet. You've promised to feed and clean its mess. They finally say yes! And you are so excited! You choose Tiger, the cat, who can't wait to move in and be the best loving cat you've ever owned. His hobbies are sleeping and playing with toys.

Tiger

Body

With Variegated, ch 4 **loosely**; being careful **not** to twist ch, join with slip st to form a ring.

Rnd 1 (RS): Ch 1, 2 sc in same ch as joining and in each ch around; do **not** join, place marker to indicate the beginning of the rnd (**see Markers, page 18**): 8 sc.

Rnd 2: 2 Sc in each sc around: 16 sc.

Rnd 3: Sc in each sc around.

Rnd 4: † Slip st in FLO of next sc (**Fig. 1, page 19**), ch 4 **loosely**, slip st in second ch from hook, sc in next ch, hdc in next ch, slip st in same st as first slip st worked (Ear made) †, sc in both loops of next sc, repeat from † to † once, sc in both loops of next 13 sc.

Rnd 5: Sc in free loop behind next Ear (**Fig. 3a, page 19**), sc in both loops of next sc, sc in free loop behind next Ear, sc in both loops of next 13 sc.

Rnd 6: (Skip next sc, sc in next sc) around: 8 sc.

Rnds 7-9: Sc in each sc around.

Rnd 10: Sc in next 2 sc, † ch 11 **loosely**, 4 hdc in second ch from hook, hdc in each ch across, slip st in same st as last sc worked †, sc in next sc, repeat from † to † once, sc in next 5 sc, slip st in next sc; finish off.

Finishing

Tack head to neck.

Use photos as a guide for shaping and for placement of features and accessories.

the Dog

Mutt, the Pup, loves his green tennis balls and scratches behind his ears. Your new Dog will welcome you home with pounces that will you make you feel like he misses you a little too much. How adorable! Do you love Mutt as much as he loves you?

Body

With Cream, ch 4 **loosely**; being careful **not** to twist ch, join with slip st to form a ring.

Rnd 1 (RS): Ch 1, 2 sc in same ch, sc in next 3 chs; do **not** join, place marker to indicate the beginning of the rnd **(see Markers, page 18)**: 5 sc.

Rnds 2-4: 2 Sc in next sc, sc in each sc around: 8 sc.

Rnd 5: 2 Sc in each sc around: 16 sc.

Rnd 6: Sc in each sc around, changing to Brown in last sc **(Fig. 2, page 19)**; cut Cream.

Rnd 7: † Slip st in FLO of next sc **(Fig. 1, page 19)**, ch 7 **loosely**, hdc in second ch from hook and in each ch across, slip st in same st as last slip st worked (Ear made) †, sc in both loops of next 2 sc, repeat from † to † once, sc in both loops of next 12 sc.

Rnd 8: Sc in free loop behind next Ear **(Fig. 3a, page 19)**, sc in both loops of next 2 sc, sc in free loop behind next Ear, sc in both loops of next 12 sc.

Rnd 9: (Skip next sc, sc in next sc) around: 8 sc.

Rnds 10-13: Sc in each sc around.

Rnd 14: Sc in next 3 sc, † ch 12 **loosely**, hdc in second ch from hook and in each ch across, slip st in same st as last sc worked †, sc in next sc, repeat from † to † once, sc in next 4 sc, slip st in next sc; finish off.

Finishing

Tack head to neck.

Use photos as a guide for shaping and for placement of features and accessories.

General Instructions

Abbreviations

BLO	Back Loop(s) Only
ch(s)	chain(s)
cm	centimeters
dc	double crochet(s)
FLO	Front Loop(s) Only
hdc	half double crochet(s)
mm	millimeters
Rnd(s)	Round(s)
RS	right side
sc	single crochet(s)
sp(s)	space(s)
st(s)	stitch(es)
tr	treble crochet(s)
YO	yarn over

Symbols & Terms

★ — work instructions following ★ as many **more** times as indicated in addition to the first time.

† to † — work all instructions from first † to second † as many times as specified.

( ) or [ ] — work enclosed instructions **as many** times as specified by the number immediately following **or** work all enclosed instructions in the stitch or space indicated **or** contains explanatory remarks.

colon (:) — the number of stitches after a colon at the end of a row or round denote(s) the number of stitches you should have on that row or round.

Gauge

Correct gauge is essential for proper size. Hook size given in instructions is merely a guide and should never be used without first making a sample swatch approximately 2" (5 cm) square in the stitch, yarn, and hook specified. Then measure it, counting your stitches carefully. If your swatch is smaller than specified, try again with a larger size hook; if larger, try again with a smaller size. Keep trying until you find the size that will give you the specified gauge. **DO NOT HESITATE TO CHANGE HOOK SIZE TO OBTAIN CORRECT GAUGE.**

Markers

Markers are used to help distinguish the beginning of each round being worked. Place a 2" (5 cm) scrap piece of yarn before the first stitch of each round, moving the marker after each round is complete.

CROCHET HOOKS																	
U.S.	B-1	C-2	D-3	E-4	F-5	G-6	7	H-8	I-9	J-10	K-10½	L-11	M/N-13	N/P-15	P/Q	Q	S
Metric - mm	2.25	2.75	3.25	3.5	3.75	4	4.5	5	5.5	6	6.5	8	9	10	15	16	19

Yarn Weight Symbol & Names	LACE 0	SUPER FINE 1	FINE 2	LIGHT 3	MEDIUM 4	BULKY 5	SUPER BULKY 6	JUMBO 7
Type of Yarns in Category	Fingering, size 10 crochet thread	Sock, Fingering, Baby	Sport, Baby	DK, Light Worsted	Worsted, Afghan, Aran	Chunky, Craft, Rug	Super Bulky, Roving	Jumbo, Roving
Crochet Gauge* Ranges in Single Crochet to 4" (10 cm)	32-42 sts**	21-32 sts	16-20 sts	12-17 sts	11-14 sts	8-11 sts	6-9 sts	5 sts and fewer
Advised Hook Size Range	Steel*** 6 to 8, Regular hook B-1	B-1 to E-4	E-4 to 7	7 to I-9	I-9 to K-10½	K-10½ to M/N-13	M/N-13 to Q	Q and larger

*GUIDELINES ONLY: The chart above reflects the most commonly used gauges and hook sizes for specific yarn categories.

** Lace weight yarns are usually crocheted with larger hooks to create lacy openwork patterns. Accordingly, a gauge range is difficult to determine. Always follow the gauge stated in your pattern.

*** Steel crochet hooks are sized differently from regular hooks–the higher the number, the smaller the hook, which is the reverse of regular hook sizing.

CROCHET TERMINOLOGY		
UNITED STATES		INTERNATIONAL
slip stitch (slip st)	=	single crochet (sc)
single crochet (sc)	=	double crochet (dc)
half double crochet (hdc)	=	half treble crochet (htr)
double crochet (dc)	=	treble crochet (tr)
treble crochet (tr)	=	double treble crochet (dtr)
double treble crochet (dtr)	=	triple treble crochet (ttr)
triple treble crochet (tr tr)	=	quadruple treble crochet (qtr)
skip	=	miss

BASIC	Projects using basic stitches. May include basic increases and decreases.
EASY	Projects may include simple stitch patterns, color work, and/or shaping.
INTERMEDIATE	Projects may include involved stitch patterns, color work, and/or shaping.
COMPLEX	Projects may include complex stitch patterns, color work, and/or shaping using a variety of techniques and stitches simultaneously.

Back or Front Loop Only

Work only in loop(s) indicated by arrow (**Fig. 1**).

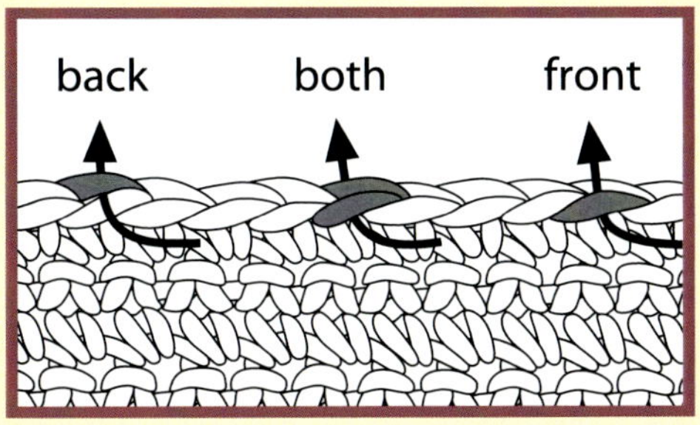

Fig. 1

Changing Colors

Work the last stitch to within one step of completion, hook new yarn (**Fig. 2**) and draw through loops on hook. Cut old yarn and work over both ends.

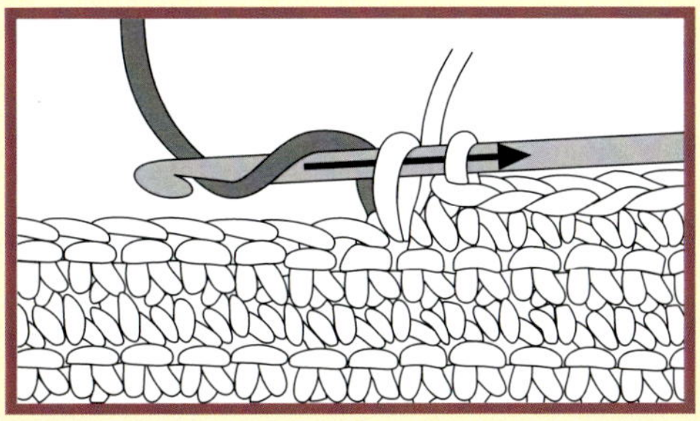

Fig. 2

Free Loops

When instructed to work into free loops of a round, work in loop indicated by arrow (**Fig. 3a**).
When instructed to work into free loops of a chain, work in loop indicated by arrow (**Fig. 3b**).

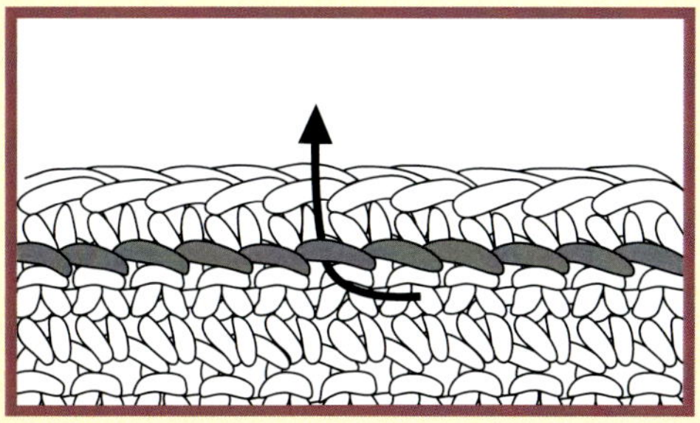

Fig. 3a

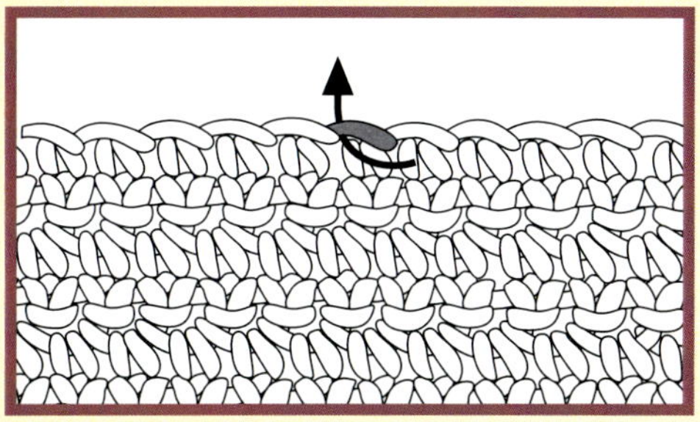

Fig. 3b

cat
dog
2
+2
4

Loop Stitch

Insert hook in next stitch, wrap yarn around index finger of left hand once **more**, insert hook through both loops on finger following direction indicated by arrow **(Fig. 4a)** and being careful to hook all yarns **(Fig. 4b)**, draw through stitch, remove finger from loop, YO and draw through all 3 loops on hook **(Loop St made, Fig. 4c)**.

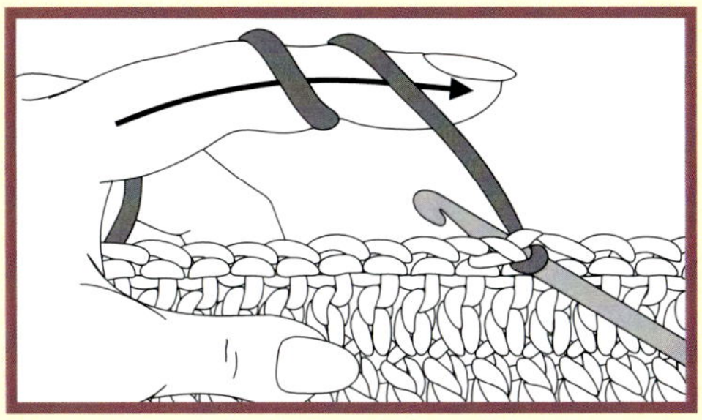

Fig. 4a

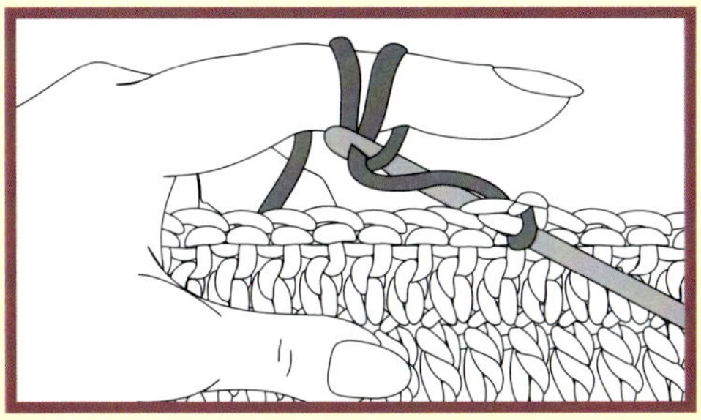

Fig. 4b

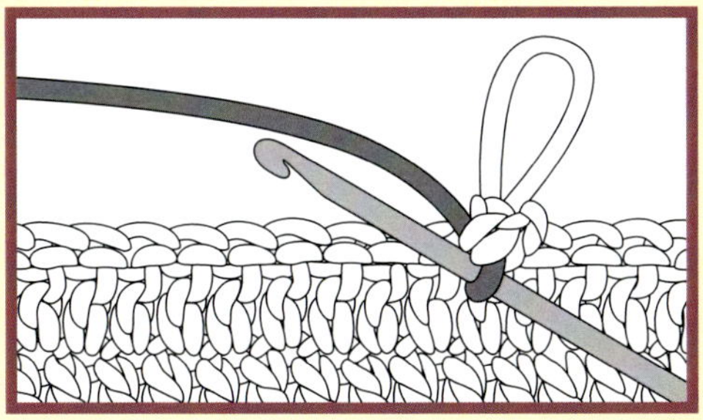

Fig. 4c

Fringe

Using a crochet hook, fold single strand in half, draw the folded end up through stitch indicated and pull the loose ends through the folded end **(Fig. 5a)**; draw the knot up tightly. Repeat as instructed. When necessary, work around post of stitch indicated **(Fig. 5b)**.

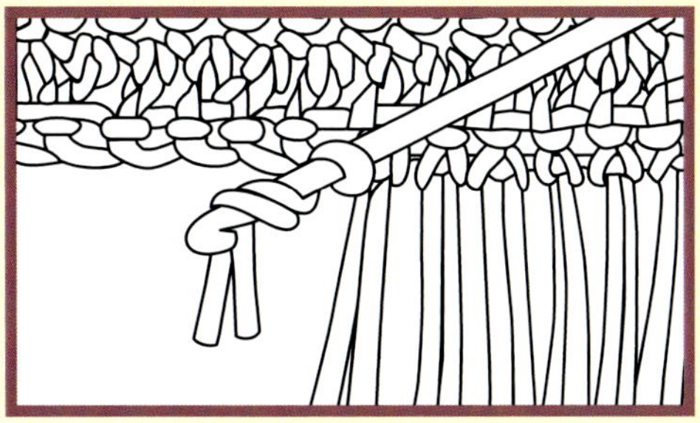

Fig. 5a

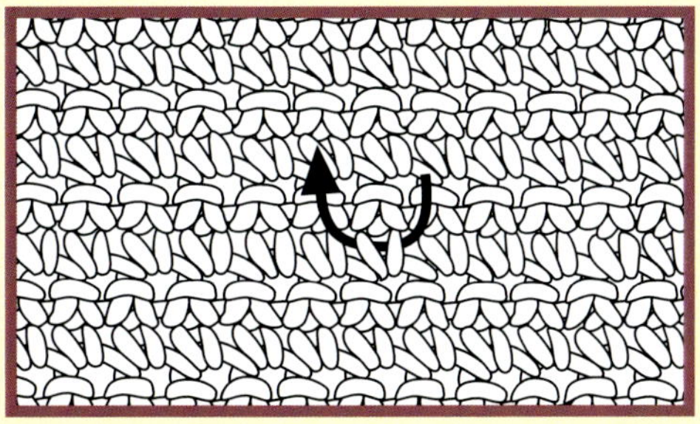

Fig. 5b

Single Crochet
(abbreviated sc)

Insert hook in stitch or space indicated, YO and pull up a loop, YO and draw through both loops on hook **(Fig. 6, single crochet made)**.

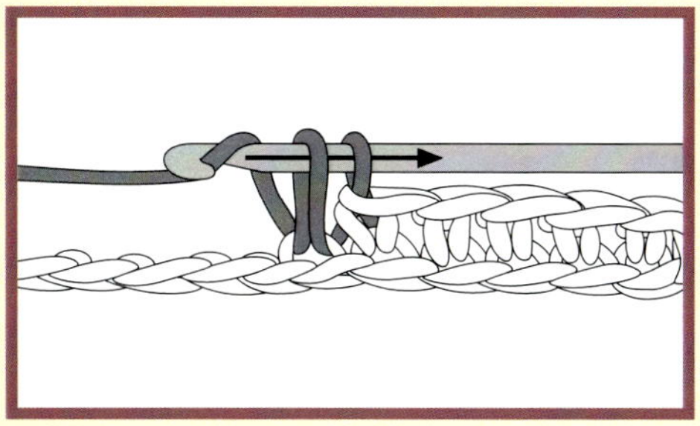

Fig. 6

Half Double Crochet
(abbreviated hdc)

YO, insert hook in stitch or space indicated, YO and pull up a loop, YO and draw through all 3 loops on hook (**Fig. 7, half double crochet made**).

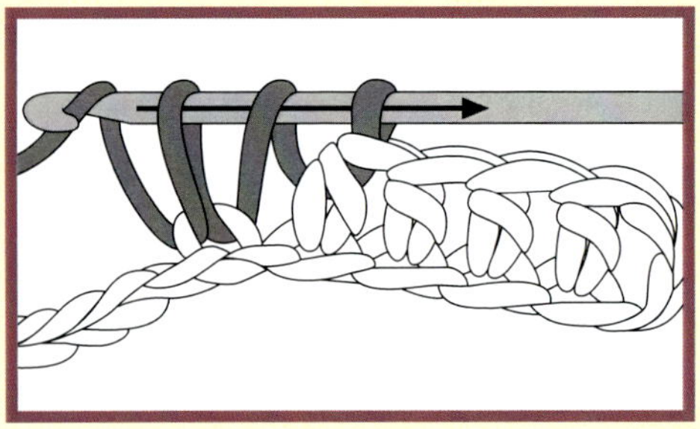

Fig. 7

Double Crochet
(abbreviated dc)

YO, insert hook in stitch or space indicated, YO and pull up a loop (3 loops on hook), YO and draw through 2 loops on hook (**Fig. 8a**), YO and draw through remaining 2 loops on hook (**Fig. 8b, double crochet made**).

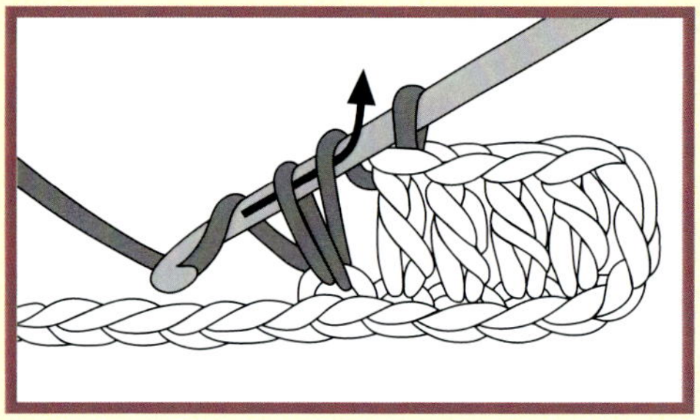

Fig. 8a

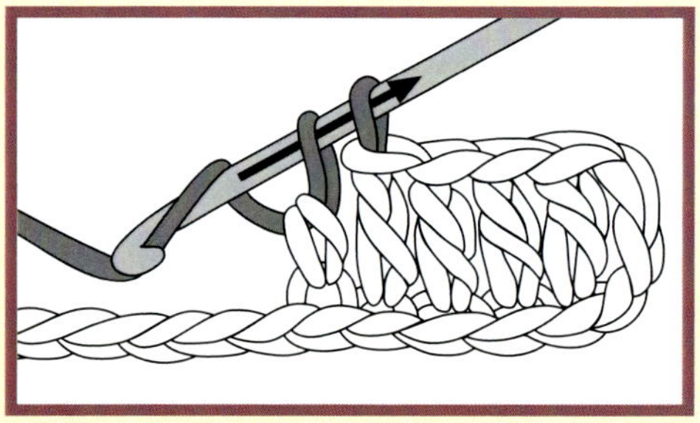

Fig. 8b

Treble Crochet
(abbreviated tr)

YO twice, insert hook in stitch or space indicated, YO and pull up a loop (4 loops on hook) (**Fig. 9a**), (YO and draw through 2 loops on hook) 3 times (**Fig. 9b & c, treble crochet made**).

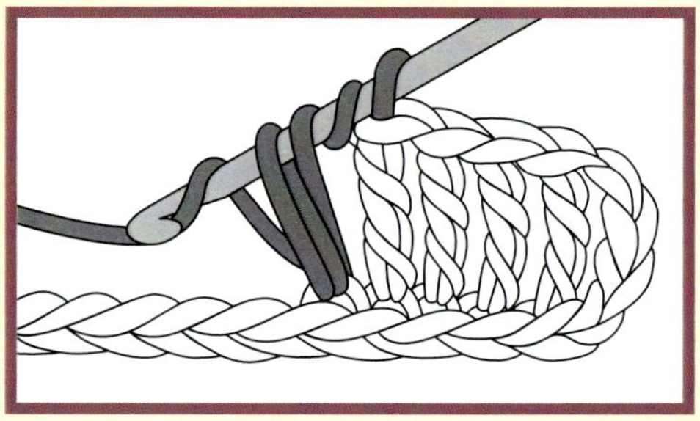

Fig. 9a

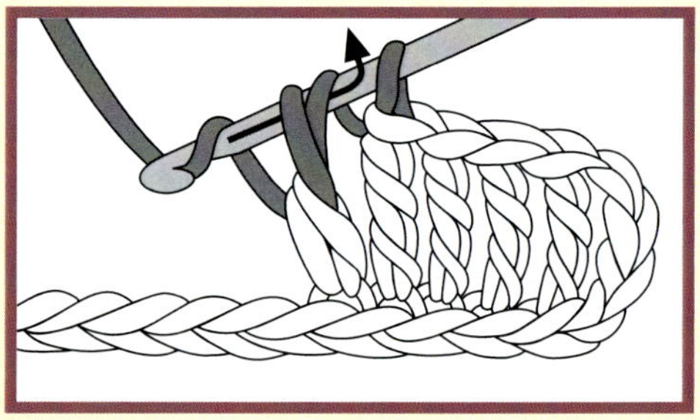

Fig. 9b

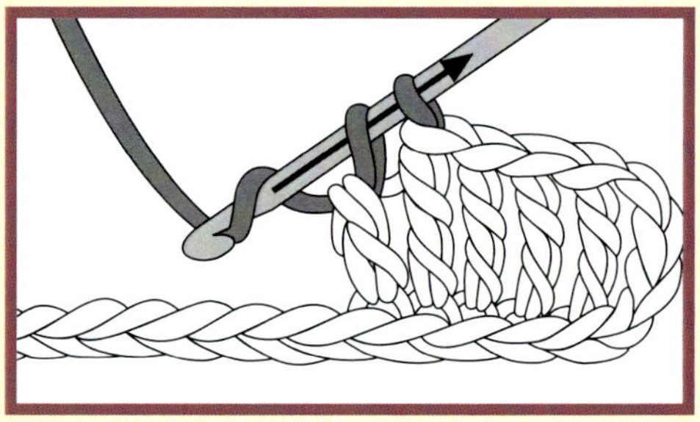

Fig. 9c

Show us what you're working on!

Share your project photos with us on social media.
Tag us @leisureartsinc or use #leisurearts

We have made every effort to ensure that these instructions are accurate and complete. We cannot, however, be responsible for human error, typographical mistakes, or variations in individual work.

Production Team: Publishing Manager - Megan Copeland; Project Manager/Technical Manager - Linda A. Daley; Graphic Artist - Michael Puckett; Photo Stylist - Lori Wenger; and Photographer - Jason Masters.

Made in U.S.A.